FIRST HYMNS

illustrated by

BRENDA MEREDITH SEYMOUR

The Lutterworth Press

First published, 1967
This impression 1991

The Publishers wish to make acknowledgement to the following for the right to include hymns of which they control the copyright: The Methodist Youth Department ("To the Baby Jesus" by Vivienne Sage); Miss M. Cropper ("Jesus' Hands were kind Hands" by Margaret Cropper);

The Lutterworth Press
P.O. Box 60
Cambridge CB1 2NT
England

ISBN 0 7188 0308 6

Printed in Hong Kong by Colorcraft Ltd

CONTENTS

To the Baby Jesus

To the Baby Jesus
Little flowers did bring
All their sweetest fragrance,
For an offering.

To the Baby Jesus
Ox and ass did come,
Offering their stable
To Him for a home.

To the Baby Jesus
All the birds did sing,
Making royal music
Fit for any king.

To the Baby Jesus
All the world shall come;
In each heart that loves Him
He shall find a home.

Vivienne Sage

I Love to Hear the Story

I love to hear the story
Which angel voices tell,
How once the King of Glory
Came down on earth to dwell;
I am both weak and sinful,
But this I surely know:
The Lord came down to save me,
Because He loved me so.

I'm glad my blessèd Saviour
Was once a child like me,
To show how pure and holy
His little ones might be;
And if I try to follow
His footsteps here below,
He never will forsake me,
Because He loves me so.

To sing His love and mercy
My sweetest songs I'll raise;
And though I cannot see Him,
I know He hears my praise.
For He has kindly promised
That even I may go
To sing among His angels,
Because He loves me so.

Emily Huntingdon Miller

Jesus' Hands were Kind Hands

Jesus' hands were kind hands,
  doing good to all,
Healing pain and sickness,
  blessing children small;
Washing tired feet, and saving
  those who fall;
Jesus' hands were kind hands,
  doing good to all.

Take my hands, Lord Jesus,
  let them work for You;
Make them strong and gentle,
  kind in all I do;
Let me watch You, Jesus,
  till I'm gentle too,
Till my hands are kind hands,
  quick to work for You.

Margaret Cropper

Through the Night Thy Angels Kept

Through the night Thy angels kept
Watch beside me while I slept;
Now the dark has passed away;
Thank Thee, Lord, for this new day.

North and South and East and West
May Thy holy name be blest;
Everywhere beneath the sun,
As in heaven, Thy will be done.

Give me food that I may live;
Every naughtiness forgive;
Keep all evil things away
From Thy little child this day.

William Canton

There's a Friend for Little Children

There's a Friend for little children
Above the bright blue sky,
A Friend who never changes,
Whose love will never die:
Unlike our friends by nature,
Who change with changing years,
This Friend is always worthy
The precious Name He bears.

There's a home for little children
Above the bright blue sky,
Where Jesus reigns in glory —
A home of peace and joy:
No home on earth is like it,
Nor can with it compare,
For everyone is happy,
Nor could be happier, there.

There's a crown for little children
Above the bright blue sky,
And all who look to Jesus
Shall wear it by and by;
A crown of brightest glory
Which He will then bestow
On those who found His favour
And loved Him here below.

There's a song for little children
Above the bright blue sky,
A song that will not weary,
Though sung continually;
A song which even angels
Can never, never sing;
They know not Christ as Saviour
But worship Him as King.

There's a robe for little children
Above the bright blue sky;
A harp of sweetest music
And palms of victory;
And all above is treasured
And found in Christ alone;
Oh, come, dear little children,
That all may be your own.

Albert Midlane

Jesus Bids us Shine

Jesus bids us shine with a pure,
clear light,
Like a little candle burning in the
night.
In the world is darkness; so we
must shine —
You in your small corner, and I
in mine.

Susan Warner

Tell me the Stories of Jesus

Tell me the stories of Jesus
I love to hear;
Things I would ask Him to tell me
If He were here:
Scenes by the wayside,
Tales of the sea,
Stories of Jesus,
Tell them to me.

First let me hear how the children
Stood round His knee;
And I shall fancy His blessing
Resting on me:
Words full of kindness,
Deeds full of grace,
All in the love-light
Of Jesus' face.

Tell how the sparrow that twitters
On yonder tree
And the sweet meadow-side lily
May speak to me;
Give me their message,
For I would hear
How Jesus taught us
Our Father's care.

Tell me, in accents of wonder,
How rolled the sea,
Tossing the boat in a tempest
On Galilee;
And how the Master,
Ready and kind,
Chided the billows
And hushed the wind.

Into the city I'd follow
The children's band,
Waving a branch of the palm-tree
High in my hand;
One of His heralds,
Yes, I would sing
Loudest hosannas:
'Jesus is King!'

Show me that scene in the garden
Of bitter pain;
And of the Cross where my Saviour
For me was slain.
Sad ones or bright ones,
So that they be
Stories of Jesus,
Tell them to me.

William Henry Parker

All Things Bright and Beautiful

All things bright and beautiful,
All creatures great and small,
All things wise and wonderful,
The Lord God made them all.

Each little flower that opens,
Each little bird that sings,
He made their glowing colours,
He made their tiny wings.

The purple-headed mountain,
The river running by,
The sunset, and the morning
That brightens up the sky.

The cold wind in the winter,
The pleasant summer sun,
The ripe fruits in the garden,
He made them every one.

The tall trees in the greenwood,
The meadows where we play,
The rushes by the water,
We gather every day.

He gave us eyes to see them,
And lips that we might tell
How great is God Almighty,
Who has made all things well.

Cecil Frances Alexander

Jesus, Friend of Little Children

Jesus, Friend of little children,
Be a friend to me;
Take my hand and ever keep me
Close to Thee.

Teach me how to grow in goodness
Daily as I grow;
Thou has been a child and surely
Thou dost know.

Step by step, O lead me onward,
Upward into youth;
Wiser, stronger still becoming
In Thy truth.

Never leave me nor forsake me,
Ever be my friend,
For I need Thee from life's dawning
To its end.

W. J. Mathams

All Creatures of our God and King

All creatures of our God and King,
Lift up your voice and with us sing:
  Alleluia, Alleluia!
Thou burning sun with golden beam,
Thou silver moon with soften gleam:
  O praise Him, O praise Him,
  Alleluia, Alleluia, Alleluia!

Thou rushing wind that art so strong,
Ye clouds that sail in heaven along,
  O praise Him, Alleluia!
Thou rising morn, in praise rejoice,
Ye lights of evening, find a voice:

Thou flowing water, pure and clear,
Make music for thy Lord to hear:
  Alleluia, Alleluia!
Thou fire so masterful and bright,
That giveth man both warmth and
  light:

Let all things their Creator bless,
And worship Him in humbleness;
  O praise Him, Alleluia!
Praise, praise the Father, praise the
  Son,
And praise the Spirit, Three in One:

St Francis of Assisi,
trans. William Henry Draper

PRAISE, O PRAISE OUR GOD AND KING

Praise, O praise our God and King!
Hymns of adoration sing:
For His mercies still endure,
Ever faithful, ever sure.

Praise Him that He made the sun
Day by day his course to run:

And the silver moon by night,
Shining with her gentle light:

Praise Him that He gave the rain
To mature the swelling grain:

And hath bid the fruitful field
Crops of precious increase yield:

Praise Him for our harvest store;
He hath filled the garner floor:

And for richer food than this,
Pledge of everlasting bliss:

Glory to our bounteous King!
Glory let creation sing:
Glory to the Father, Son,
And blest Spirit, Three in One.

Henry Williams Baker

Saviour, Teach me, Day by Day

Saviour, teach me, day by day,
Love's sweet lesson to obey;
Sweeter lesson cannot be,
Loving Him who first loved me.

With a childlike heart of love,
At Thy bidding may I move;
Prompt to serve and follow Thee,
Loving Him who first loved me.

Teach me all Thy steps to trace,
Strong to follow in Thy grace;
Learning how to love from Thee,
Loving Him who first loved me.

Thus may I rejoice to show
That I feel the love I owe;
Singing, till Thy face I see,
Of His love who first loved me.

Jane Eliza Leeson

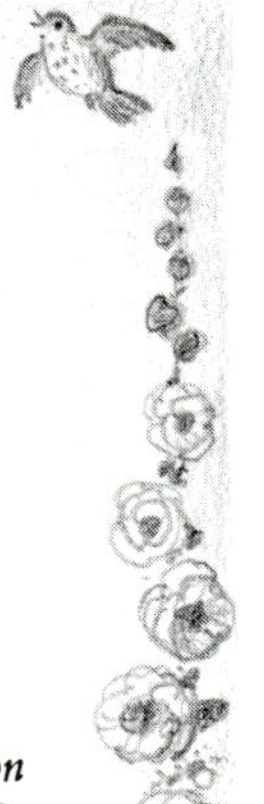

We Plough the Fields, and Scatter

We plough the fields, and scatter
The good seed on the land,
But it is fed and watered
By God's almighty hand;
He sends the snow in winter,
The warmth to swell the grain,
The breezes and the sunshine,
And soft refreshing rain:

All good gifts around us
Are sent from heaven above;
Then thank the Lord, O thank
the Lord,
For all His love.

He only is the maker
Of all things near and far;
He paints the wayside flower,
He lights the evening star;
The winds and waves obey Him,
By Him the birds are fed;
Much more to us, His children,
He gives our daily bread:

We thank Thee then, O Father,
For all things bright and good,
The seed-time and the harvest,
Our life, our health, our food;
Accept the gifts we offer
For all Thy love imparts,
And, what Thou most desirest,
Our humble, thankful hearts:

Matthias Claudius
trans. J. M. Campbell

God, Who Made the Earth

God, who made the earth,
The air, the sky, the sea,
Who gave the light its birth,
Careth for me.

God, who made the grass,
The flower, the fruit, the tree,
The day and night to pass,
Careth for me.

Sarah Betts Rhodes

There is a Green Hill far away

There is a green hill far away,
Without a city wall,
Where the dear Lord was crucified
Who died to save us all.

We may not know, we cannot tell,
What pains He had to bear;
But we believe it was for us
He hung and suffered there.

He died that we might be forgiven,
He died to make us good,
That we might go at last to heaven,
Saved by His precious blood.

There was no other good enough
To pay the price of sin;
He only could unlock the gate
Of heaven, and let us in.

O dearly, dearly has He loved,
And we must love Him too,
And trust in His redeeming blood,
And try His works to do.

Cecil Frances Alexander

O Jesus, I have Promised

O Jesus, I have promised
To serve Thee to the end;
Be Thou for ever near me,
My Master and my friend!
I shall not fear the battle
If Thou art by my side,
Nor wander from the pathway
If Thou wilt be my guide.

O let me feel Thee near me!
The world is ever near;
I see the sights that dazzle,
The tempting sounds I hear;
My foes are ever near me,
Around me and within;
But, Jesus, draw Thou nearer,
And shield my soul from sin.

O let me hear Thee speaking
In accents clear and still,
Above the storms of passion,
The murmurs of self-will!
O speak to reassure me,
To chasten or control;
O speak, and make me listen,
Thou guardian of my soul!

John Samuel Bode

Praise God, from Whom All Blessings flow

Praise God, from whom all blessings
  flow;
Praise Him, all creatures here below;
Praise Him above, ye heavenly host;
Praise Father, Son, and Holy Ghost.

Thomas Ken